Permission to Grieve

How To Cope Through Public Loss In The Midst of Private Pain

Dwann Holmes

Permission to Grieve

How To Cope Through Public Loss In The Midst of Private Pain

Copyright © 2021 by Dwann Holmes

Published by GICMP PRESS

All rights reserved. This book or parts thereof may not be reproduced in any form, stored in any retrieval system, or transmitted in any form by any means— electronic, mechanical, photocopy, recording, or otherwise—without prior written permission of the publisher, except as provided by United States of America copyright law. For permission requests email publisher via Media@GlobalPropheticInstitute.com

ISBN: 978-1-7366119-0-6

DEDICATION

This book is written in honor of my father Dewayne Holmes Sr. (April 1948- January 2016.) and his mother, my grandmother Eleanor Nash Holmes (May 1913 - March 2015). This book is also dedicated to my immediate family, my mother Lillie, my brother Dewayne Jr. (Dee) my sisters Kandi & Karmen (KarKar) and those who have struggled with grief when they least expected to, simply because you didn't know the power of loss. May you be empowered to recognize the importance of effectively grieving your way through whatever situation comes your way. And may you find comfort and confirmation in the words written on the pages of this book.

Table of Contents

Acknowledgments	i
PREFACE	iii
INTRODUCTION	x
PERMISSION TO GRIEVE	1
GRIEF IS A PROCESS	9
Summary and Analysis	13
Pastoral Care and Applied Theology	13
Deliberate Theology (Your theological perspective)	14
Pastoral Care as Applied Psychology (Psychosocial Issues)	15
HELPING POINTS!	17
MY GRIEF PROCESS	30
Analysis of Self (Self Supervision):	44
GRIEF CONTINGENCY PLANNING FOR LEADERSHIP	49
GET CLARITY	50
ALLOW HUMANITY	53
GRIEF AND TRANSITION FROM ONE CHURCH TO THE NEXT	58
COVID-19 AND GLOBAL GRIEF	65
Prayer for Your Leader	74
PRAYERS FOR GRIEF AND RECOVERY	74
Prayer for Anyone Walking Through Loss of a Loved One	75
Prayer for Anyone Who Has Experienced Unexpected Job Loss	76
Prayer for Anyone Going Through Separation or Divorce	77
Global Prayer for Our World	78
The Serenity Prayer (Author Unknown)	79
GRIEF PHOTOTHERAPY	80
Worley Wedding Photos	83
A Legacy of Service	84
A Century Fulfilled	85

ACKNOWLEDGMENTS

First, many thanks to Prophet Shani Brown whose thought-provoking questions and transparency made me realize that a book on grief from a new perspective might be a good idea.

Thanks to Chaplain Scott Fleming & Chaplain Scott Speight my instructors who provided valuable insight and instruction that helped to lead those in the chaplain cohort I participated in via Transitioning Pathways, LLC. and Memorial Hospital (Memorial Health) where department head Chaplain Larry Glover had the awesome vision to launch and host Clinical Pastoral Education (CPE)

I must also take the time to salute my fabulous Lead Graphic Designer of GICMP and ChurchDesignsNow.com & BizDesignsNow.com

Thom Sagun who always helps me birth my media vision with great excellence and precision.

Also a huge THANK YOU to Photographer Bryant McCain, Inner Soul Images who did a spectacular job creatively capturing the photos and video from my father's memorial service and funeral and burial. Last but not least, thanks Prophet, Dr. Marilyn Weekes for editing.

PREFACE

One of the best decisions I ever made was to enroll in Clinical Pastoral Education (CPE) and Training otherwise known as Chaplaincy Training. In the beginning, I don't think I ever imagined the depth of what I would learn about myself and others by simply taking that first step to enroll when given the opportunity.

Though most, probably, have heard and seen the volunteer chaplains who appear to roam the halls of hospital hallways or can fondly reflect on sports chaplains who appear to motivate teams spiritually, I believe there are a vast numbers of folk who have goals of professional certification, yet don't understand the amount of training that goes into official CPE

I pulled this detailed description from my Supervisor's Report compiled after my first unit completion. Here's how Scott Fleming of Transitioning Pathways, LLC put it via one of my assessments:

The program consisted of 400 hours of clinical training and ministry. The unit ended with four students in an extended 20-week unit of CPE. The CPE group was conducted using a web-based interactive conferencing system with one meeting in person. Participants, including the Supervisor, were in Florida. The unit incorporated transformational learning theory and Family Systems theory in its provision. The unit focused on a variety of topics and discussions. Various didactic sessions include but are not limited to:

Psychological First Aid

> *Innovations in Family-Centered Approaches to Trauma and Loss*

Use of Self in Pastoral Care and Counseling

> *Theological Reflection as it Relates to CPE Curriculum*

Active Listening

Spirituality and Trauma

Guided Conversation

Developing Cultural Competencies in Spiritual Care

Grief and Depression

The students read and discussed multiple articles that were directly related to their research interests and pertinent to their learning goals. This strategy was intended to allow the students to take final responsibility for their own learning while also seeking to round out their own desired learning for the unit. Students were engaged in this process and encouraged to allow these articles to inform them in their clinical work.

Throughout the unit, each student presented verbatims, meditations, or theological reflections. They also submitted written weekly reflections and participated in individual supervision, peer- to-peer conversations, and group supervision on a regular schedule. Sociograms were submitted by the students every four weeks during the program. Students had the option of writing a mid-unit evaluation should they so choose.

Wow! See what I mean.

CPE takes its trainees purposely on emotional rollercoasters meant to better the student's perspective of learning while serving people in the midst of a health crisis.

Sooner or later, though, in the midst of helping someone in crisis, you will find yourself doing so during your own personal crisis, as well.

Such was the case for me, when my father died just a month before my CPE Unit began.

Exactly 30 days to the date before my CPE Unit began, I flew back home to Omaha to check on my father Dewayne Holmes Sr. Thirty days later, my father died of heart failure, January 27, 2016.

Somehow, though, he hung on long enough to walk his baby girl, my sister Karmen Worley down the aisle 4 months earlier in September 2015.

Dewayne Holmes Sr. was a proud Father.

I've learned a lot about love, life, family and a father's love since he's been gone.

I've learned even more about grief.

And yes, it's true, you never know how much you miss a person or what you value the most about them many times until they ARE gone.

I think what I miss the most is his authentic love and support of who God called and assigned me to be.

The truth is, I've learned through him, Love is indeed an ACTION WORD!

Thus, believe what people do above what they say until their actions meet and live up to their words.

Though he didn't say "I love you!" much growing up because that was his culture and I'm good with that, he did ALL he could to show love through his loving actions.

He was actually on my ministry email list and would respond back to my emails when I would least expect it.

I don't even think I knew he had registered to be on it until he responded to one of my email updates.

I remember the time I shared about an event I hosted where God moved in signs, wonders and miracles!

His email response was

"You know your great-grandmother was a healer too! Even in the Baptist church in Louisiana! "

I was flabbergasted!!!

How could he have not remembered to share that earlier?

He had never shared that verbally or anything of the sort.

Yet, via email he was able to connect me with a glimpse of my spiritual heritage!

Also, at least once a month or so, he would make sure to have my mother send a donation from what came in his household.

No matter how many times he made sure to send it, I was always pleasantly surprised and honored at the same time!

Nope, that wasn't about the money, it was about the fact that he clearly recognized and received the God in me enough to sow into me.

Indeed there is nothing like the affirmation of a FATHER.

So for all the ways he took time to affirm and bless me in peculiar ways in his latter years, I honor him.

INTRODUCTION

Several years ago, after the death of my father, I was talking to one of my prophetic mentees Shani Brown, about the grief process and how it affects leaders.

It was interesting to hear her perspective: "Leaders never really get the chance to grieve in private, it's always public."

The more I thought about that, the more I agreed.

In March 2015 my paternal grandmother Eleanor Holmes Nash died at the age of 101.

In January 2016 her son, my dad, Dewayne Holmes Sr. died at the age of 67.

I was honored to deliver both Eulogies never imagining they'd come so close together.

Some thought, though I delivered my grandmother's I may not want to deliver my father's.

They thought it might be "too much"

But what I knew was that just like my dad asked me to deliver my grandmother's eulogy, he would want the same for himself.

So, on February 5, 2016 on a cold, dreary, snowy day in Omaha, Nebraska at Salem Baptist Church we celebrated my dad's life and I released the Word: "The Miracle In Death: I MADE IT!"

Two weeks later, I was ready to go through my own grief process and I knew as a multi-faceted leader, I had to be careful and willing to walk through whatever I needed to walk through to guarantee healing.

As I mentioned, I thank God that at that same time, I was enrolled in my first unit of Clinical Pastoral Education (CPE) for Chaplaincy which helped me tremendously sort through my feelings as I reflected on self via our assignments.

I also thank God for the spectacular prayer warriors

assigned to me who didn't fall off the wall or walk away when they were needed most.

Prayer makes a difference!

I was also happy to make frequent trips back to Omaha and to have photos and videos that I could watch while reflecting on the memories of my loved ones. This also served as therapy for my mind, spirit and soul.

To this day I will pull out videos of the dynamic Omaha Mass Choir who sang during my dad's funeral and musical celebration.

It brings me so much joy, even when I shed a tear or two.

Yet, if I were to attempt to lend a helping hand of advice for those who are Marketplace Leaders, Ministry Leaders or Senior Pastors who are walking through the process of grief, here's how I would put it:

WHEN GRIEF HITS YOUR PULPIT

When Apostles, Prophets, & Pastors Grieve

Give them time to breathe

Give them time to cleave

Give them permission to cry,

To talk,

To be silent,

To ponder

To slow down

To speed up

To be themselves without questioning "WHY?"

Give them time to LEAD with YOU reflecting on THEIR actions and results from the past that can help your future.

Give them your loyalty, your love and your leadership in doing so while not allowing the balls they normally carry to be dropped.

Give them your commitment to guard them even in their humanity without judging their words and lack-there-of.

Give them time to hurt.

Give them time to heal.

Give them time to hope.

Give them the courtesy to be honest and the kindness to help.

Give them time to reflect on their loss without losing you and your attention simply because offense has outweighed your discernment to see what is NOT being said.

Give them the same GRACE you want extended to YOU when crisis hits your home!

That's, essentially, what I want to attempt to share, namely, How to handle personal pain in the midst of your public crisis and how to help others get through grief when it feels like you don't know what to do.

1

PERMISSION TO GRIEVE

I don't think I ever would have imagined that I would be releasing a book on grief in the midst of a global pandemic. However, I honestly believe this is how providence works. At a time when grief is at an alltime high, it just so happens that this guide book on grief is available to all. As you're reading through these pages keep in mind that the vision and the inception of this book project started well before Covid-19. So I'm hopeful anyone dealing with grief or helping someone else through grief may find helpful information here.

Remember that my vantage point is that of a bi-vocational Pastor and leader of leaders and mentor of mentors. What I am sharing is what I've learned in the midst of my grief and also what I've learned in helping others grieve. Whether in the hospitals or within the walls of the church or even outside in the global marketplace, grief is grief. And grief will hit you like a ton of bricks when you least expect it, no matter how prepared you think you are! No matter how much you plan for it and no matter how much counseling you may go through, what I have found is that grief many times, may put a wrench in our plans.

Nevertheless, it is so important to make sure that in our global society we recognize each person grieves differently. What works for one person will not necessarily work for another. What turned out to be effective in helping one person cope may actually be a trigger for disaster for another person.

When my father died, I knew I wanted to document everything visually. I hired a media team to not only record his funeral services but to also document via photography as well. I knew eventually I would want to document for some sort of media presentation.

But I also knew it would serve as therapy for me during my grief process. Many times early on I would sit and listen and watch the service. Especially the choir medleys that included some of my father's all-time favorite songs. He was a minister of music for 30+ years in Omaha and a musician since he was three or four years old. So music was a part of his life and a part of our household. We just got used to going to sleep with him playing the piano in the basement until the early morning hours.

So documenting everything was so important to me and wasn't just about that moment. It was about capturing the moment for later and for therapy. However, in officiating some funerals I've had other families who never ever wanted to even see a picture of their loved one in a casket. Let alone record it.

That would be offensive to them and definitely not a way for them to grieve!

However, in my family it was what we did and what we do. For both my grandmother and my father we created memorial books with their photos and documenting the services so that at any given time we could open up the book and review.

Yet, I realize for some families who are different than my family, this would trigger a whirl wind response that they may not be able to recover from.

There's one instruction that's vital for everyone who finds they are in the midst of losing a loved one. It is to simply and purposely give yourself permission to grieve.

As such, it's also important to give our leaders, our pastors, our mentors, permission to grieve, as well giving them permission, we can't try to control how they grieve or how long they grieve. One of the most devastating things to happen to me when I was grieving my father and, now that I think about it, my grandmother, simultaneously, was to find out years down the road that someone else in leadership had told my congregation, where I was Executive Pastor, not to speak with me and to just leave me alone during the grief process.

I learned that person had given the instruction as if it had come from me, but that wasn't the case. In doing so, without discussing plans with me first, that leader made my grieving process uncomfortable for those I served. This made it harder for me because the things that some of them may have wanted to do to help assist me through grief, were essentially banned. Without me even knowing it, they were now tip-toeing around my grief. That's not how I wanted it, nor planned it. Quite frankly, I didn't plan to be in this situation. I had never been in this situation before.

So, to a certain extent I didn't know what I didn't know. And most definitely, I wasn't sure how grief would manifest in or around me. However, because I was grieving there were certain things I didn't notice and wouldn't have noticed because… I was grieving.

Yet, in this situation as I reflect back, I do remember it was an awfully "quiet" and somber time for me and had someone just taken the time to ask me how I wanted to grieve or what I did or didn't want to happen, I'm sure there would have been less broken relationships triggered by death.

When I think back, I think most of the time I was

pretty baffled because of trying to figure out within my mind how my father could die at 67, not even a year after we buried his mother, my grandmother Eleanor Holmes, otherwise known as Momo, at the age of 101.

When I did her eulogy I included my research that I found about centenarians, those who live to be 100. So for me it was the most strange thing realizing that my father essentially lived less than both of his parents when many years earlier, God had healed him of cancer. Here's a portion of what I stated as I delivered my grandmother's eulogy at her hometown church in Winnfield, Louisiana.

"In 2005, the US Census Bureau estimated the country would have 114,000 centenarians by the year 2010. The actual number reported in the 2010 census was less than half that amount at exactly 53,364 people. - out of 309 million people in the U.S. in 2010 only .0173% lived to be 100!

And that's exactly what we celebrate today!

There is a 38% probability that at least one of your ancestors was a centenarian. "

However the most recent stats as I'm finishing research in 2021, say that those numbers have almost doubled.

By the year 2018 there were 93,927 people who lived to be at least 100! HMM! AND THEN CAME COVID-19 to the U.S. in 2020!

Wow!

So according to my theory, I did not think it strange to expect that since my dad's mom was a centenarian, he would at least live past 67!

Or at least 70 the number of years we are promised on earth by our God.

But again, I had to accept the fact that this wasn't the case for my dad and I had to accept the fact that no matter how much he said he wanted to live or how much we wanted him to live or how much we even thought he would live to enjoy life with my mother in retirement, things had changed.

Life has a way of changing your plans when you least expect it.

And when grief is involved, it is hard to say or even

determine what your life will look like down the road, depending on the level of grief you're experiencing.

Keep in mind, grief is deep sorrow, especially, grief that is caused by someone's death.

2

GRIEF IS A PROCESS

If there is one thing we have truly learned in the midst of Covid-19, it is that life is precious. We've also learned that in an instant life can be gone. One moment, you're talking to a friend or family member and then in days and sometimes in hours, they're gone. In situations like this we are all faced with trying to cope in the most difficult of circumstances and cope in times of grief that we never quite imagined.

As of January 26, 2021, 2.16 million people have died from covid-19, worldwide according to Our

World In Data. This means millions are trying to cope with loss and grief.

Loss is the state or feeling of grief when deprived of someone or something of value.

No matter who you are, there's a high likelihood that right now, you are dealing with some sort of loss in your life. The question now is, "How Do You Properly Cope With Loss?" And how can you help others cope properly by simply giving them and yourself permission to grieve?

To begin, you have to realize that grief is a process that involves different levels of coping. Coping is dealing effectively with something difficult. And yes, that's easier said than done. Many times when people and families are dealing with grief, displaying effective coping mechanisms doesn't seem to enter the picture, easily.

I'm of the opinion that most people don't want to deal with death. Most people don't want to deal with the loss of a loved one. Most people don't want to deal with the loss of a dear friend or even a valued employee or partner in ministry. But the more you keep living, the more you will eventually have to deal with the pain of loss.

In times like these, I believe you have to inwardly give yourself permission to speak your own words of hope and comfort over yourself to help maintain the goal.

A great place to start is: "I WILL COMMIT TO COPE!"

Yes, make a commitment to cope and hope at the same time.

Now remember, I'm a spiritual person, so when I have to process through anything, my faith and my God play a strong part. So as I began to ask God, what coping looks like from a spiritual perspective, the answer was: Coping *is being purposeful in dealing with something difficult while still looking towards destiny!*

The definition of commit is to carry into an action deliberately. It also means to bind a contract to or committing something to something or it's a pledge. And what I have found while advising and counseling people during crisis is, though they want to get out of the situation many times the reason they remain in a specific situation so long is because they will not commit to cope.

The truth is that in order to commit to cope, you have to admit that something's wrong.

In order to commit to effectively dealing with a loss, you've got to admit that something in your life needs to be dealt with.

I remember dealing with an elderly dementia patient and her main caregiver, her daughter, during my shift at the hospital during CPE. Though they were there for a fall, it was clear to me after my visit, that they really needed access to services and maybe even help dealing with the loss of her mom's mind. It was clear she was missing that part of her mother. But from my perspective it was also clear that they needed a deeper level of help coping because there may not have been a full acceptance quite yet of how difficult it really was.

I'm going to share my Summary And Analysis of this case:

Summary and Analysis

Analysis of Person(s): The adult daughter seemed to dote on her mother as though she were a child. She seemed to be very reflective of past times and also maybe a bit preoccupied (for lack of better term) with the fact that her mother had dementia and may not really comprehend the conversation although the PATIENT MOM was clearly engaged and zoning in on me and the conversation.

Pastoral Care and Applied Theology •

Embedded Theology - Adult daughter definitely was a believer and seemed to be settled in the current situation as just being a part of life or a stage of life that takes place when parents get older. She shared information regarding her faith. As I began to pray, I immediately noticed tears coming down the eyes of the ELDERLY PATIENT MOM, even though she had dementia. That in itself made me believe that INDEED ELDERLY PATIENT MOM also had a strong faith system whether or NOT she fully understood.

Deliberate Theology (Your theological perspective)

Though I know and believe that indeed as believers ALL THINGS DO WORK TOGETHER FOR OUR GOOD. During this visit, I had to seriously ponder how that was so or could be so with this current patient and her family. It was clear the daughter was a woman of faith and it was clear that her mother was an avid church goer when she was capable of doing so. But at this point, I would think seeing her mother in that state would still cause some bouts or what I call "struggles of faith." I remember watching my grandmother's mind deteriorate in certain ways due to dementia and Alzheimer's.

I remember watching my father care for my grandmother for roughly 20+ years eventually being forced to put her in a facility because of her blindness and declining mind. But despite all of that, it seemed as though my grandmother NEVER forgot her faith nor her God at the moment you brought it up. When the deacons came with communion, though she may tell them off in one moment, she was happy to partake in the holy sacrament the next. So I can imagine the roller-coaster ride this patient's family may have been on from one day to the next, not quite understanding how one who had and/or has such a strong faith could now exist in a world created by a God who knows and creates all, yet would allow this specific situation, that technically should still or could still work together for the good.

Pastoral Care as Applied Psychology (Psychosocial Issues)

Though Adult Daughter seemed to be a woman of faith and strength, her constant need to apologize for her mom's dementia made me wonder whether or not some sort of counseling for caregivers of adult parents and/or caregivers of those with dementia might be in order and helpful. In the midst of situations like these, I believe all too often believers begin to neglect their well being and even their state of mind simply because they may not know all that is available or simply because they may choose to allow their faith to carry them in ways that aren't necessarily the best options. Depending on how much time Patient Mom has with them on earth, I believe some sort of clinical counseling for the family will be in order. Integrated Summary – All in all I believe this particular visit though fairly positive could've been much better had I taken the time to dig a bit deeper with the caregiver at that moment. Though I could relate because of the dealings I had with my paternal grandmother during my family's years of seeing her transition from an astute teacher and bible scholar to a stoic and some times combative dementia patient who lived to be 101 years old, I know there was much I probably didn't go into simply because I wasn't sure exactly which way to go. Had I taken the time to really inquire more about how the caregiver was doing and how long this had been her routine, I'm sure I could have presented at least viable options that she and others could use in the near future after leaving the hospital. Though they were there for a fall, clearly dementia was a serious concern and on the forefront of all that was being done for and with the Patient MOM. I mean what do you do, when the one who used to take care of you, you are now taking care of? How do you really know that you're doing the right thing and handling specific care needs when the patient doesn't appear to be able to really communicate all that is taking place in their bodies.

HELPING POINTS!

Would love to know about and have readily available resources for those caregivers of dementia patients and learn how to truly get to the heart of the problem when it's not as obvious as it could be.

Now, let me be clear! Just because something needs to be dealt with doesn't mean that it's your fault that something has happened. So many times when trauma comes and you go from a high to a low, as you're trying to figure out what has happened and why it has happened, you neglect to commit to coping through it. Then you wonder why you're not making any progress in this difficult time.

It may be that you haven't considered that you might be grieving. And neither has anyone else acknowledged this or given you the verbal permission to grieve, that so many people need to hear, from someone dear.

You think you're further along in the grief process than you are especially when a destiny door is right in front of you, but you can't seem to walk through. As you begin to wonder why, the process of grief begins to unfold and reveal the toll it's taken.

For some, it's long sleepless nights, for others it's not only losing sleep, but losing rest and losing friends. Yet, unfortunately you haven't begun to say: I need to commit to coping because I need to recognize that I'm living through loss.

Loss isn't just about death. Loss comes when you begin to feel grief for something that is no longer in your life that once held value. So if you're used to certain things happening all the time and all of a sudden God allows you to lose that great job that provided you a level of protection in your life, you will feel grief because of that loss.

What I heard after my father died and as I was walking through helping others grieve, was simply: "You need to grieve."

So, I had to admit, just like I had advised others in the past and as I was advising others now, to admit the thought that I'm living, and I'm also grieving.

Being purposeful about grieving meant I had to learn how to cope with loss the best way that suited me.

Catch this. No matter how much someone else claimed that a certain way of grieving was best for them, it didn't mean it was best for me.

Likewise, what I enjoy or the thing that may uplift me while I'm grieving may literally send someone into a mental health fit.

For instance, I can watch videos from my father's homegoing and get my praise on. Someone else may watch a video of their loved one over and over, and get overly consumed, spending most of their days and nights watching a video that takes them into depression and out of touch with life, so much so that they seem to never move forward for weeks. Knowing all of this, I had to truly allow myself to go through the process of grief and recovery.

While Dr. Elisabeth Kubler - Ross pioneered the work of identifying the 5 emotional stages that a dying person may deal with: denial, anger, bargaining, depression and acceptance there is much confusion at times regarding the grief process due to how some have chosen to apply this concept to death and other aspects of emotional loss.

As such some think there are 4 to 12 steps in the grief process. I'm not going to take the time to debate this. However, I will share with you, what I've experienced and what I've seen others experience during grief. Of-course I learned these and lived them out in a more in-depth way, while going through CPE.

The process of grief for me were:

- **Shock**

- **Pain.**

- **Anger** (depending on the circumstances of the death or broken-relationships with the one who had died).

- **Depression.**

- **The upward turn.** ...

- **Reconstruction and working through.** ...

- **Acceptance and hope.**

First for me in the grief process was dealing with the shock of the matter. Death or sudden loss is so shocking many times you're going back and forth between denial and shock. You're bargaining with yourself in your mind. You're telling yourself, "Oh my goodness! I can't believe this happened!" To a certain extent, you are paralyzed by the pain even though you're living with the grief in the midst of grief.

Second for me in the grief process was the pain and, sometimes, even guilt. Because of the shock of this thing, the pain has been so hard to deal with. You literally now, begin to wonder if there was anything you could have done to change the circumstances. You begin to take on the guilt even if there is no clear evidence that you could have done anything to stop this fate. You experience pain, like you've never experienced before.

Questions and statements like these, flood your mind:

Maybe I made the wrong decision.

What if this would have happened?

What if this could have happened?

Maybe it would have turned out a different way!

Then thirdly, after the pain and guilt, you begin to get mad even, angry. If you're vocal, people notice you're angry and people attribute it to your recent loss. Yet, depending on how you display this anger, some may, in your mind overstep their bounds, simply because they are trying to help.

You're so mad, you're bargaining with yourself and trying to bargain with God for another outcome that can't come forth. In the midst of your loss and in the midst of your grief, you're just angry. "Oh God, if you just allow me to be blessed one more time! God, if you would just turn this thing around."

However, the only problem is, the way God's going to turn it around, doesn't equate to what you are viewing in your head, because after all, you're grieving. And your reality doesn't match what may be going on in your mind. You are clearly in the midst of loss and at a loss.

Fourth, depression appeared to set in, even though I'm not prone to be depressed. Depression, reflection, and loneliness appeared to come together. You may begin to get so depressed and begin to reflect so much on your loss that now, you have literally taken your place, your mind, yourself, into a place of isolation.

and loneliness. You may begin to wonder why you're so lonely, not being able to recognize that this grieving process has pushed you into this place, because God allowed this person, this pet, this "significance in your life" to leave, and maybe even to vanish, without an official good-bye.

Just like that!

And yes more questions.

Can anybody else begin to feel this?

Can anyone else feel or see how I cringe on the inside?

Can anybody else begin to nurture me?

So no matter how much you want somebody else to

help, what you don't know is that you isolated yourself so much that even when people try to help, they can't help.

Yes, it may be making much more sense now that I'm taking the time to explain it and lay it out. I can tell you what I know because I spiritually advise so many people during the loss of a loved one. Not just those I Pastor but also those I may come in contact with through my prophetic chaplaincy lines.

So I began to ask, God, why can't people see what I and others see what they're doing and how they are showing up during their grief and in their loss.

By that I mean, why do people say they want help, but when you offer help, they reject it? And why do folks who are spiritual just tend to say "pray about it" without necessarily offering more help or even recognizing that maybe, just maybe, grief counseling is needed? Why are certain communities not willing to admit that grief can also trigger emotional and mental set-backs that need more than prayer?

As I pondered these questions and thoughts, I also

observed the spirit of grief nearly take certain people completely out. They couldn't identify the process and how the process was impacting them nor could they recognize how grief was literally changing them for the worse. They were consumed with grief to a point if you stayed around them too long, it would almost spill over and consume you.

Have you ever been there before or observed this with someone you know has experienced the loss of a loved one? This is when you literally have to find a way to help them find their permission to grieve before they get stuck in a whirlwind of devastating emotions they can't dig themselves out of. They keep reflecting on what used to be in such an unhealthy way until it becomes their reality. They are now living in the past so much that progress towards the future disappears. Hope isn't just deferred. It's gone.

It's a false reality because what used to be is no more. And so because of that, people won't admit where they really are and are not.

And as you probably know by now, when you don't deal with depression and loneliness, you may never get back on your upward spiral. That's because after the depression, after the loneliness, and after the reflection was when, all of a sudden, I found the release of something new.

Enter stage 5, the Upward Turn. All of a sudden what looked like darkness begins to shine as a little light at the end of the tunnel. God begins to bring back to your remembrance who you are, even if the person you thought would be with you forever, is no longer around. Providence sets in, as none other than the protective care of God to spiritually care for you and set-things in order when it appeared that all hope was lost.

When you finally accept where you are and you begin to hope again, you begin to see the bigger picture of how far from yourself you had gotten due to loss and possibly not effectively coping. God begins to remind you of who you are and you begin to accept this thing and hope your way through this thing for the Stage 6 and 7 the process of reconstruction and hope to take place.

But again, you cannot accept where you are, if you don't admit where you are. you cannot accept where you are if you don't admit where you are, where you are not and where you need to go.

Until you understand the process of grieving or what it will take to effectively cope, things may just seem like they're at a standstill. But I believe God does a deep work in your soul as you find that sweet spot in your coping process. That sweet spot is when healing truly comes and you are no longer consumed with the death or the loss. It's at this point that you should do, what I call: SUBMITTING TO COPING.

You have to be willing not just to just commit to coping but to submit to the process of coping until you can begin to truly manifest a life that flourishes. You have to be willing to yield to that counselor, that spiritual advisor or that process that is clearly beneficial to your sanity and to your ability to live with others peaceably.

Now time for one of my famous sidebars, lol. Right after I was divorced by my girls' father, my college sweetheart whom I literally thought I would be with for the rest of my life, I experienced a kind of grief I had never experienced before. But it wasn't until 3 to 4 years afterwards that I could really reflect on the devastation of the divorce while also assessing how the loss affected my ability to grieve or not grieve.

I was coping and I was doing all I knew to do to move forward but I realized afterward, that my bed had become my best friend. And to a certain extent my bed had become my girls' place of refuge and safety as well. I was a functioning depressed person and prophet. Somehow, I was still able to help others experience their breakthrough when clearly, I needed one as well.

But I was depressed and didn't know it! Because the prophet in me still stood up supernaturally. So in the midst of my situation, when things were going crazy, the prophet was still being pulled on and was still able to minister to people.

I was still able to negotiate media contracts and was presented with one of the best coaching/consulting contracts ever. But I would be so tired when I would get up. I never seemed to be at full energy level. And I was still busy trying to make ends meet because eventually it got to a point where child-support was little to nothing. However, I knew two little girls who were depending on me to get up so I got my butt up out the bed morning after morning. I had a decent enough support system, but for whatever reason, I never heard anyone around me explain that I was grieving.

That never dawned on either me or them.

All I knew to do was to fast and pray. That's when prayer and fasting truly became another level of lifestyle for me. And then God used my dear friend Karen Swim to say to me: "Dwann, the shame is not yours to carry!" It was like supernaturally God gave me beauty for ashes. He literally turned my darkness to light instantly!

Yet, throughout the process, I was in sporadic counseling. It wasn't until after the counseling and after the heartfelt words of a friend, that I truly conquered that type of grief and began to live again.

It wasn't until my dad died many years later, that I was able to now understand what grief looks like during different situations of loss.Plus, I was able to comprehend that though there are 7 stages of grief, the process of grieving in order to effectively cope, may look very different depending on the situation of loss.

MY GRIEF PROCESS

I'm sure my grief process looked very strange to some. The week that my father died I still ministered and held mentorship sessions for those in my prophetic mentorship program. I was almost done with 30 days of Prophecy which had started the first of January 2016. So I pushed through and finished as I felt that was the best thing for me to do. I went to church that Sunday as well which was in Georgia that particular Sunday. Though I was weeping, that's where I wanted to be, sunglasses and all.

In My Mind and Spirit my goal at that moment was to simply get through to the other side of the funeral. So that meant from my perspective I could officially start my grieving process after February 5th.

I decided to take 30 days to purposely work

through my grief and my emotions knowing that I still had much to do in the year ahead. So that meant I had to really focus on myself, my mental health and my well-being.

I was encouraged by this scripture which explains David's process of grief:

2 Samuel 12

The Death of David's Son

And the Lord struck the child that Uriah's wife bore to David, and it became ill. 16 David therefore pleaded with God for the child, and David fasted and went in and lay all night on the ground. 17 So the elders of his house arose and went to him, to raise him up from the ground. But he would not, nor did he eat food with them. 18 Then on the seventh day it came to pass that the child died. And the servants of David were afraid to tell him that the child was dead. For they said, "Indeed, while the child was alive, we spoke to him, and he would not heed our voice. How can we tell him that the child is dead? He may do some harm!"

19 When David saw that his servants were whispering, David perceived that the child was dead. Therefore David said to his servants, "Is the child dead?"

And they said, "He is dead."

20 So David arose from the ground, washed and anointed himself, and changed his clothes; and he went into the house of the Lord and worshiped. Then he went to his own house; and when he requested, they set food before him, and he ate. 21 Then his servants said to him, "What is this that you have done? You fasted and wept for the child while he was alive, but when the child died, you arose and ate food."

22 And he said, "While the child was alive, I fasted and wept; for I said, 'Who can tell whether [b]the Lord will be gracious to me, that the child may live?' 23 But now he is dead; why should I fast? Can I bring him back again? I shall go to him, but he shall not return to me."

Reading this scripture gave me so much confirmation and peace. While my father was alive, I had done what I knew I needed to do to acknowledge what appeared to be his increasing heart failure. That's why I flew to Omaha, just 30 days before he died. At that time I didn't know he would be gone so quickly. However, I did hear concern in my conversations with both my parents.

I thank God that I was able to get there before he passed away. I also thank God that I was able to take him to one of his last doctor appointments to really get insight on next steps on dealing with his heart issues.

He was on an oxygen tank and anytime he took it off, you could hear how much he struggled to breathe. I didn't really notice the severity until that day I drove him and my mother to the hospital for his doctor's appointment. Panic almost set in, as he kept saying he was having a hard time breathing. As I'm driving I hear my mom trying to console him, but I don't think anyone can ever understand what that type of illness "feels like" or does to you mentally without ever experiencing it on your own.

Even as I heard him speaking with as much intrepidity as possible, I could sense the fear. And it was during those moments that I had to tell myself, this was way more serious than I imagined.

Reflecting back, there was even talk about the LVAD Heart Pump (Left Ventricular Assist Device). He had driven to Lincoln, Nebraska about an hour away, to see if he was a candidate. Even though he and my mother were given hope, as I read more about his circumstances, including age, that possibility seemed out of sight ,especially, after learning how non-thrilled he seemed about the possibility of living with some mechanical contraption. After all he had a pacemaker installed years ago.

Though he won his bout with cancer of the blood, (Leukemia) all of the treatments really did impact his heart. So by the time December 2015 got here, I really just wanted to know his thoughts on living longer and see for myself how much prayer and fasting might be warranted.I needed to know for myself if we needed a miracle.

Of course he wanted to live. Of course he felt he had more to do on earth. After all, he was only 67. Yet his heart capacity had gotten all the way down under 20 percent. That was bad!

REALLY bad!

Yet, once he died, I knew my life couldn't and wouldn't just come to a halt. Though I was ready to truly mourn after his burial, I still found hope knowing that he had made it to the other side, as I had proclaimed during his funeral.

So, I gave myself 30 days to just do what I needed to do for me. I live a reclusive life, so finding time to myself and being by myself is no problem. Stealing away even within a home full of people is easy for me. During this time, I reviewed all the photos and played the videos of my dad's memorial concert over and over. I enjoyed listening to the full sound of the choir. I enjoyed hearing what his mentees and colleagues had to say about him. It brought much gratification.

During this time, I also worked on his memorial photo book. And the final solace was knowing that indeed when he fought through cancer and lived, I truly believe God added to his life, just like He did when Hezakiah prayed.

2 Kings 20

In those days was Hezekiah sick unto death. And the prophet Isaiah the son of Amoz came to him, and said unto him, Thus saith the Lord, Set thine house in order; for thou shalt die, and not live.

2 Then he turned his face to the wall, and prayed unto the

Lord, saying,

3 I beseech thee, O Lord, remember now how I have walked before thee in truth and with a perfect heart, and have done that which is good in thy sight. And Hezekiah wept sore.

4 And it came to pass, afore Isaiah was gone out into the middle court, that the word of the Lord came to him, saying,

5 Turn again, and tell Hezekiah the captain of my people, Thus saith the Lord, the God of David thy father, I have heard thy prayer, I have seen thy tears: behold, I will heal thee: on the third day thou shalt go up unto the house of the Lord.

6 And I will add unto thy days fifteen years; and I will deliver thee and this city out of the hand of the king of Assyria; and I will defend this city for mine own sake, and for my servant David's sake.

God didn't just give my dad 15 years he gave him 27 years. He was diagnosed with leukemia during the Thanksgiving season of 1989. Then in the first quarter of 1990, my baby sister was diagnosed with a cancerous tumor on her bladder. She was just 1.5

years old. As my mother had given birth to her on her 40th birthday. Knowing all of this gave me perspective.

God also saw fit to allow my dad to walk his baby girl down the aisle to get married and to jovially tell her to "multiply" right before the daddy-daughter dance.

All of that brought so much joy to him. He had a long marriage of more than 45 years with his elementary school hometown love and 4 grown children and 7 grandchildren. Plus, he had also sacrificed to make sure his mom, who was blind, was well taken care of in the years that she needed to be cared for.

He had lived a full-life.

I mourned, but I celebrated and honored his memory and legacy knowing it would fuel me to also make sure I move forward accomplishing what I still needed to accomplish in life. There was nothing more that I could do except LIVE FULL.

Again the great thing for me was that I was in the beginning stages of my clinical pastoral education.

Fortunately for me, I was able to continue through with it, until I completed the last unit, Unit 4 near the end of December 2017.

In late 2016 I presented the theological reflection during my CPE class. I will share that with you at this time.

"One year ago during the weekend of September 18th 2015, I was in my hometown of Omaha, Nebraska celebrating the marriage of my youngest sister Karmen with my family and friends.

Then (4) Months later, I was back in Omaha Eulogizing my father, who died at the age of 67, exactly 30 Days to the day of my last quick-trip back to Omaha to assess what was really going on with his health.

It was a rough start to the year of 2016 for me and my family.

Though we knew he was sick we didn't anticipate death at that moment, so soon.

Nevertheless I'm thankful that God in his infinite Wisdom gave me many opportunities in the latter part of my father Dewayne's life to talk with him frequently, to minister to him, to pray with him and to be a voice of reason to him when at times he may not listen to others.

I'm honored that God also graced me to deliver his Eulogy in the midst of those who loved and cared for him.

Yes, his legacy doesn't just live on in me and my family, it lives on in the FOUNDATION I created in HONOR OF HIM and the music he so adored.

He walked and lived in purpose and didn't question what God assigned him to do on earth.

So I stand with that same confidence knowing that indeed, every aspect of the work I'm doing now in 2016 and beyond, God ordained.

Whether we understand it or not, it's in LIFE'S uncomfortable and unusual circumstances that I believe we as BELIEVERS come closer to DESTINY.

As I always say, in the midst of a crisis, we have 2 choices. To draw closer to DEATH or closer to DESTINY ... knowing that indeed GOD allows all things to work out for our GOOD.

As pastors and leaders in the body of Christ, sometimes it's challenging to take the time to assess ourselves, our feelings and the results of our own situations when we give so much to others.

Yet, no matter how much we give to others now more than ever as we choose to allow God to continue using us for HIS GLORY, via CPE, it's imperative to make sure that we understand when He's working things out for our good, how we can HINDER that process if we don't take the time for much personal reflection, personal assessment and personal QT."

It was during this time of study and helping others through health crises including death that helped me to heal as well. The group sessions with the other students in CPE also served as therapy as we all had to deal with personal obstacles that might hinder our progress during CPE. As a matter of fact, there were some who couldn't make it through, or chose to not move forward because of the intensity of the level of study and application. Also, of course along the way, there seemed to be more death of those I once was close to during different stages of my life.

Because I did much of my work online and within the global community, I was fortunate to be able to use some of those situations as case studies that helped me and my colleague and instructor see where I was and where I wasn't.

During CPE it is so important to be willing to be transparent not just with yourself but with those you serve. You have to be willing to take your emotional guards down in order to serve patient clients best.

You have to be able to admit, when something personal that you are going through or have gone through may help you serve your patients best. However, if your guard is up and you are not willing to be transparent regarding where you are in life, you may be projecting on your patients as much as they may be projecting on you, and your CPE journey may not benefit you at the level it could and should.

And yes, you have to also be willing to be vulnerable enough to allow your emotions and discernment to help you, not hurt you.

CPE clinical case reports are delivered via a specific format.

- **Background**
- **Pastoral Plans**
- **Impressions and Observations**
- **Pastoral Conversations**
- **Summary and Analysis**
- **Analysis of Person(s)**
- **Analysis of Self (Self- Supervision)**
- **Embedded Theology**
- **Deliberate Theology**
- **Pastoral Care as Applied Psychology**
- **Integrated Summary**

In early 2017 one of my former mentees Wynesha Joy Medley was murdered. She was like a part of my family, as we had opened up our house to her in the midst of her transition from Daytona to Jacksonville, as she was trying to figure out what to do next in life.

She was a free-lance graphic designer working

towards building her business and brand and was allowed to stay in my guest room.

During that time, we worked closely and she shared her dreams and aspirations before deciding to move on to Savannah to be near her sister.

As a graphic designer she was a digital midwife of dreams for so many ministry and marketplace leaders whose ideas she brought to life. Though it had been months, since I had spoken to her, after speaking with her mother to offer my condolences, her mother followed up with me later and asked me to do the eulogy and burial.

She also asked me to reach out to a young man who had commented on the post that I released to acknowledge Wynesha's death.

She gave me some specific words to say to him from her.

I won't share that, but I will share portions of my summary and analysis from this case study that I created to present to my CPE cohort.

Analysis of Self (Self Supervision):

This was a tough one because I knew in the midst of the situation everyone was looking for someone with spiritual authority to speak up and say something.

Thus I had no choice but to write a heartfelt tribute on my ministry page.

That tribute seemed to help many flush through their feelings and reach out to me in a way they may not have reached out to others.

Yet, even the weight of being "that" person still seemed to push me forward to make sure that those in need could find a listening ear. I knew speaking to this young man was important to Mentee's mom, so I pushed through any pain I may have had at the moment to really serve one who I felt needed to be served. Plus, this time, I talked to Mentee's mom which was a bit of healing for me. So I was good with what was going on.

I know doing this would help in my goals to learn how to merge Pastoral Counseling with CPE from a learning perspective.

EMBEDDED THEOLOGY - *Client's relationship with God means a lot to him. He seemed to draw a lot of* strength in his faith, by hearing from his mother as well. She seemed to be a matriarch of faith.

Growing up, much of what I learned and believed regarding God and what he allows and doesn't allow came from the 2 matriarchs of my family, my mother and my paternal grandmother. No matter what the catastrophe was, we were always taught God was in it and working it out for our good. No matter how crazy or illogical it seemed. We just knew if we held on to God's unchanging hand, we would be alright.

I recall my father and 1.5 year old sister both had cancer at the same time and both were in chemotherapy at the same time. That was one of those times in my life where I learned to just lean on God in prayer and TRUST that even if I didn't understand how a loving God could allow this, He still was worth believing in and trusting through the chaos.

That happened when I was a freshman in college at age 18.

Though it was trying, it was when I really went to another level of faith and fortitude and learned about the power of prayer and how God can and will sustain you even when you can't explain fully the power of your faith *and your faith in God.*

I've always held on to this and believed this foundation helped me tremendously while dealing with the tragedy of losing a mentee to murder and, then also, at the same time, having to pastor her family and friends even in the midst of my grief.

DELIBERATE THEOLOGY– *IN the word of God, one of the 10 commandments is THOU SHALT NOT KILL.*

For those of us who are believers, I think it's hard to understand and comprehend how people of faith can get caught up in situations that lead to murder.

Studies show that most murders are not random killings.

They happen in the heat of a moment or they happen to folks who know each other.

Yes, random killings happen but how often do we really know someone who's been killed? How do we as chaplains and leaders position ourselves to serve and walk others through this type of situation, when you believe and others believe that truly they've done the right thing to live a life that wouldn't cause them to go out like this.

Yes, unbelievable, when you learn that lots of killings like this are acts of passion and abuse. Then you begin to wonder how could someone so strong and bright become a victim of domestic violence and how can we as a church and as leaders of believers help to identify when and if it's happening close to home and in our congregations or organizations.

Do we have what it takes to identify it? What does the bible say about sounding the alarm and how to help save one from such devastation ?

Pastoral Care as Applied Psychology – *The client really seemed to be fixated on the fact that maybe he could have rescued mentee from this situation. I will follow up to have another conversation to see if any counseling is needed.*

Integrated Summary: Still processing all that has transpired and still wondering how else I may have to be used in this situation. Death is hard enough, but when it's the death of a young person via murder and labeled domestic violence, I feel it becomes even more challenging.

So many unanswered questions about the cause of death can be very daunting, not just to the family but yes, even to those of us called to serve the family and friends.

Nevertheless, I'm always honored when God gives me an opportunity to represent Him as I help others come to a place of peace in the midst of their grief and, yes, even mine.

3

GRIEF CONTINGENCY PLANNING FOR LEADERSHIP

As a leader, you have to realize that no matter what, those you lead, expect you to lead all the time. Whether you're in the midst of a crisis or not feeling well, yourself, those you lead expect that you will lead them to victory by any means necessary. Typically, that may mean even if you are neglecting yourself and your family to serve them.

As Pastors, it's hard for us to see someone we are assigned to shepherd, going through. It's hard to not get involved and help when you know you can.

However, during your personal and many times public crises as a leader, it is so important to provide clarity regarding what should happen when and if you find yourself in the midst of grieving while leading.

I believe it's best to have a grief contingency plan organized and discussed with your core leadership so they know how to maneuver in the midst of your pain. Make sure as you're grieving you are willing and able to give clarity, to all levels regarding where you are during your grief process.

GET CLARITY

Within this grief contingency plan, identify how your leaders can get clarity to help serve those you lead, in the midst of your grief.

So we are all clear, there are different levels of clarity that will be needed as you grieve. Clarity is the quality of being coherent and intelligible. And simply put, clarity means, to be clear. We know that grief ushers in a range of emotions and cloudiness. So, I truly believe the leadership team has to go out of it's way to get clarity, especially, if you're not clear.

If you're clearly not sure about what to do or how your leader wants to grieve or plans to grieve, you have to find a way to communicate and have that conversation.Yes, though it may be hard and challenging, you have to understand in the shell-shock of grief, though you may see your leader moving forward and even leading, during the grief process, it's also important to talk to your leader about how he or she would like to grieve.

Be honorable, yet direct.

Ask if there is something they need.

Ask how often your leadership team should "touch-base" with him/her.

Ask if there is something they feel they're not getting.

Ask if there are triggers that they are aware of.

Ask if they need to take a break and if so, how long. Better yet, suggest that they take a break but be willing to have an operational plan that clearly demonstrates what will happen in their absence so they will be confident that they can take a break.

No matter how big or small the organization, leaders, particularly Pastors don't skip breaks and vacations because they want to, they skip many times because they're not confident the ship will keep moving forward at the level they know they require .

Even if there are standard operating procedures in place and even if staff and volunteers have been trained properly, we all know, in the midst of a crisis many times, systems collapse when those procedures and plans aren't implemented.

Don't be afraid to have that candid, yet calm conversation to make sure in the midst of a leader's grief, they are still able to have the space they need while also having the engagement they need as well. No one has the right to speak on behalf of your leader unless they've truly been given that delegation and it's been made clear.

However, I can not stress enough how much different people grieve different ways. Different people have different expectations during the grief process. In the long run, false delegation and sincere yet misguided instructions will only cause more harm and confusion than clarity. You can not have clarity without proper communication.

Unless someone has talked to your leader and has definitely heard from them first hand, you can not assume how grief will and won't affect them, no matter how close you think you are to them.

ALLOW HUMANITY

In preparing a grief contingency plan, no matter how strong you think your leader is, you must allow room for their humanity in the midst of their grief process. Yes, I admit, I am seen and known as a "strong black woman." However, I also understand that being seen as strong can also be a "curse" as well.

Strong people tend to be the ones overlooked the most in the midst of grief. Strong people tend to be the ones you label as "able to handle anything" whether the crisis is death or divorce. Strong people, even when they verbalize needing help or wanting help tend to be ignored or not allowed to be human, more so than anyone else.

One of the most hurtful things that happened to me in the midst of my grief was when one of my top leaders in my global ministry submitted her resignation within 60-90 days of my father's death.

No call to discuss an exit plan.

No call to discuss her transition.

Just a seemingly random letter via email, explaining her new plans, which didn't include the organization she had promised to help me lead into the future. I was doubly devastated.

Not completely surprised though because I believe God always gives leaders an indication of the hearts of the people they serve. However, as a human being who has feelings, I was hurt.

In one moment this person had sent me the most thoughtful care package, days after my father died, which truly soothed my soul and spirit but within 3 months she was putting in her notice and hadn't talked to any of our team leaders to get advice on the best way to do so in the midst of my grief. Nor did she take the time to have a conversation with me.

Do you see how this could add to the grief?

I'm not saying stop your life and don't do what you think you need to do to progress in life, when your leader is grieving. What I am saying is remember that your leader is a real person, with real feelings.

No matter how much you've seen them strongly lead others during someone else's personal crisis, during your leader's bout with the public crisis of losing a loved one, please don't forget they are real people. Please don't forget, they too will have to go through the 7 steps of grief like any other grieving person. This is when you have to give your leader permission to grieve the most.

As you give them permission to grieve, it's important to familiarize yourself and your organization with what that looks like from a clinical perspective.

This means to a certain extent familiarizing yourself with the 7 steps of grief as well. As stated earlier they are:

- *Shock.*
- *Pain and guilt*
- *Anger and bargaining. ...*
- *Depression. ...*
- *The upward turn. ...*
- *Reconstruction and working through. ...*
- *Acceptance and hope.*

Be sure you and other leaders know what it may look like when your leader is exhibiting characteristics of grief that may be mislabelled which then may lead to mishandling of your leader's pain.

- *Reduced concentration*
- *A sense of numbness*
- *Disrupted sleep patterns*
- *Changed eating habits*
- *Roller-coaster of emotional energy.*

These characteristics are all present when most people experience grief. However, one of the main goals should be to help your leader get to a point of grief recovery that is more than just manageable.

According to "The Grief Recovery Handbook, 20th Anniversary Edition" by John W James & Russell Friedman" recovery from loss is achieved by a series of small and correct choices made by the griever." The book goes on to state that "unfortunately most of us haven't been given the proper information with which to make the correct choices."

But that doesn't have to be your fate if you're in the midst of the grief journey nor does it have to be the fate of your leader if you know they are clearly walking through a major loss.Position yourself to be a solution for grief recovery. Position yourself to get equipped regarding what that might look like.Now more than ever as the whole world is experiencing record high bouts with grief,a true plan of recovery is indeed needed for all.

4

GRIEF AND TRANSITION FROM ONE CHURCH TO THE NEXT

Every year, I counsel hundreds of prophetic voices about how to transition from one spiritual house to another. I was getting so many inboxes, that I created a webinar entitled: How to Transition Right As a Prophet. That webinar can be found via my prophetic institute website at GlobalPropheticInstitute.com

Sometimes they listen.

Sometimes they don't.

Sometimes they get mad.

Other times they're glad.

I realize now much of how they feel and how they react also has a lot to do with their grief process. Unfortunately, when it's time to leave a church many have not been given permission to grieve or even told that they will need to.

Here's what I call: *The Truth About Grief & Transition from One Church To The Next*

A few years back at an awards nominee luncheon I listened as one of the nominees spoke of needing a new church home, because after so many years in ministry and pastoring, her beloved Pastor decided to close the church.

You could tell even though she understood, she was in the midst of transition struggling to find a spiritual place to call home and more. Later, when she asked me for my card, I began to speak from my heart.

"As you search for a home, keep in mind you just need a place to sit in the back if need be or where-ever you feel led and cry and grieve," I shared.

"Yes!" She agreed. "It really feels like losing something!" she continued.

"You did lose something. You loss your spiritual home that you had been a part of for years. You lost the Pastor you came to love! So it really is like experiencing death!" I explained.

"You are right. I just was talking to someone about this the other day!"

As we continued the conversation, I explained how God had given me the term Spiritual Foster Care for those like her in the midst of transition.

Her eyes widened as she listened intently.

All too often I come across many in transition from one church or organization to the next, who haven't taken the time to grieve or identify the process they are in. Whether it's a forced transition like the one I mentioned above or a planned exit created by the one leaving, the fact of the matter is, there will be grief.

Here again, as the pandemic has forced believers to do church differently, there are many churches that didn't make the cut. There are many churches that have closed and there are many sheep who are lost in the field or still trying to figure out what to do, in the midst of this pandemic transition of loss.

Unfortunately, we almost never hear about the grief we experience when it's time to leave a church, or, even a long-time job.

Yet, it does exist.

And it's happening now, like never before. On January 27, 2021 the U.S. Bureau of Labor Statistics reported : "From March 2020 to June 2020, gross job losses from closing and contracting private-sector establishments were 20.4 million, an increase of 12.6 million jobs from the previous quarter, the U.S. Bureau of Labor Statistics reported today. Over this period, gross job gains from opening and expanding private-sector establishments were 5.7 million, a decrease of 1.2 million jobs from the previous quarter. The difference between the number of gross job gains and the number of gross job losses yielded a net employment loss of 14.6 million jobs in the private sector during the second quarter of 2020."

Yes, you read this correctly.

This also adds to what I call the global grief in the land.

It's a loss.

When we are truthful with ourselves, whether it's moving from one church to the next or even going from on-site worship to digital worship, or yes, losing a job, we'll be able to identify that the feelings and emotions we experienced while in transition, really can be labeled, "GRIEF."

Though all don't necessarily go through the same process of grief, it's pretty much the same as most common theories explain:

There are the "symptoms" that you experience right after the loss, even when you are happily searching for a new spiritual home.

- Shock and disbelief

- Sadness

- Guilt

- Anger

- And, yes, physical symptoms as well, like loss of appetite, weight-gain, pains, aches and, yes, even insomnia.

During this time of transition, it's important to be able to recognize where you are and land somewhere people will allow you to go through the process of grief even in your new spiritual home or temporary home.

Fact is: it happens even when the transition is a "happy" one, like those that come with new marriages, new job transfers etc ... Yep, it's happened to me too.

Back in the day, while growing up in Omaha, Nebraska I remember hearing about watch-care when people joined churches while in a city temporarily. While living in Nashville, Tennessee I saw lots of college students take advantage of watch-care.

Now days, we offer this type of care at Global Prophetic Life Training & Worship Embassy the prophetic hub known as #GPLJAX here in Jacksonville, Florida for those believers in transition.

We call it FOSTER-CARE, so those in transition know and understand they can connect in covenant with a temporary place to call home while they are being healed and experience grief, without being or feeling forced to commit or over-commit too soon.

The truth about transitioning from one church to the next, is it can hurt more than you anticipated simply because you never imagined, this type of grief.

5

COVID-19 AND GLOBAL GRIEF

According to the Centers for Disease Control and Prevention there are unprecedented effects of grief and loss due to COVID-19

"Some people may experience multiple losses during a disaster or large-scale emergency event. Because of the COVID-19 pandemic, you might be unable to be with a loved one when they die, or unable to mourn someone's death in-person with friends and family. Other types of loss include unemployment, or not making enough money, loss or reduction in support services, and other changes in your lifestyle. These losses can happen at the same time, which can complicate or prolong grief and delay a person's ability to adapt, heal, and recover."

And it's these losses that are mentioned throughout the CDC's website that confirm for me what I've observed locally and globally.

There really is global grief all over the world due to the losses triggered by COVID-19.

However, because many of us as leaders may not be able to verbalize what we are seeing from the church to Corporate America to even colleges and universities, it's been challenging to provide the right type of support.

If you're not used to observing someone who is having a mental breakdown you may quite possibly label them as just having a hard time or even losing their mind, without recognizing the need to try to get them some immediate clinical help.

Fortunately for me I have those on my leadership staff who deal with significant mental health issues on a regular basis at their day job. And we have had different families who also have had to deal with mental health issues within their families in the past that have been helpful in helping identify when those we serve may need more than we are able to provide.

During the day I work at my Educational Institute, GICMP, which trains ministerial leaders across the globe. At GICMP we also have Outreach prayer lines that function 5 days a week, plus a prayer line that people can call into and simply leave a message regarding their prayer concern.

Recently while reviewing a message via our phone lines, that was left by a young lady in the Atlanta area, one of our staff Prophets was able to identify that this young lady needed a possible intervention. Her message was full of ramblings and strange commentary regarding what another prayer team in Atlanta was trying to do to her mind.

I believe she called us because of the credibility of our Marketplace Ministry. She was desperate for help and desperate for prayer. But after the right people reviewed the message it was determined that someone needed to go a step further and potentially reach out to the college that she said she was a part of and also give her a call to see if there were any family members close by who could be of assistance to her.

She was clearly having a mental health breakdown.

For whatever reason, the best option for her was calling our prayer line even though we were 5 hours away.

This incident only reconfirmed what I had shared with my leadership team and what I believe I see happening to regular churchgoers and to those happy-go-lucky employees who find themselves stuck at home.

Human engagement is necessary for human beings.

Spiritual encouragement and nourishment that used to take place at churches across the globe are sorely missed.

Whether you're used to interacting with your families at Sunday brunches and dinners hosted after church, or, you're used to monthly work team gatherings, they all made a difference in the lives of people who now find themselves struggling to just cope.

And unfortunately when they feel as though they can no longer cope they may turn to extreme circumstances and risk their lives and those of their family members just for human interaction.

I'm not sure how many Houses of Hope or corporations are offering grief counseling or grief recovery to their communities even for the ones who may not have experienced the death of a close loved one. If it's not being considered or not being suggested, I truly believe it should be considered. It could make a huge difference. Yes, even at schools across the country and the world as well.

Here's how the CDC has described adolescent grief.

"Adolescents may also experience grief in ways that are both similar to and different than children and adults. Adolescents may experience significant changes in their sleep patterns, isolate themselves more, frequently appear irritable or frustrated, withdraw from usual activities, or engage more frequently with technology. It is important for parents or caregivers to engage with their adolescents over their grief to promote healthy coping and acceptance. Parents may also need to obtain mental health services for the adolescent and family to deal with grief."

Now more than ever, we have to also pay attention to our children and encourage them to express themselves. In addition, we must do what we can to help provide sanity in the midst of this new normalcy that is hard to comprehend even for adults.

When school started in 2020, I decided to keep my teenage daughter home rather than allow her to go to school. I wanted to make sure her school and our district had a handle on protecting their students. So, for this whole first semester she did online school. I could clearly see how this new way of learning was impacting her livelihood, her spirits, and even her classes. Now, she's back in school and of course we have daily conversations on safety and homework. However, I am a bit amazed that even over these first couple of weeks, I can clearly see a change in her demeanor. There's been an upward shift if you will allow me to call it that. The human interaction with her friends does make and has made a difference. And of course my constant prayer is that God will continue to keep her safe.

Here are more instructions from the CDC:

"If you feel distress from other types of loss or change

During the COVID-19 pandemic, you may feel grief due to loss of a job; inability to connect in-person with friends, family or religious organizations; missing special events and milestones (such as graduations, weddings, vacations); and experiencing drastic changes to daily routines and ways of life that bring comfort. You may also feel a sense of guilt for grieving over losses that seem less important than loss of life. Grief is a universal emotion; there is no right or wrong way to experience it, and all losses are significant.

Here are some ways to cope with feelings of grief:

- Acknowledge your losses and your feelings of grief.

  - *Find ways to express your grief. Some people express grief and find comfort through art, gardening, writing, talking to friends or family, cooking, music, gardening or other creative practices.*

- Consider developing new rituals in your daily routine to stay connected with your loved ones to replace those that have been lost.

  - *People who live together may consider playing board games and exercising together outdoors.*

  - *People who live alone or are separated from their loved ones may consider interacting through phone calls and apps that allow for playing games together virtually.*

- If you are worried about future losses, try to stay in the present and focus on aspects of your life that you have control over right now.

Helping children cope with grief

To support a child who may be experiencing grief:

- *Ask questions to determine the child's emotional state and better understand their perceptions of the event.*

- *Give children permission to grieve by allowing time for children to talk or to express thoughts or feelings in creative ways.*

- *Provide age and developmentally appropriate answers.*

- *Practice calming and coping strategies with your child.*

- *Take care of yourself and model coping strategies for your child.*

- *Maintain routines as much as possible.*

- *Spend time with your child, reading, coloring, or doing other activities they enjoy. "*

6

PRAYERS FOR GRIEF AND RECOVERY

Prayer for Your Leader

Dear Lord,

Thank You for my leader, (Name of Leader)

Please bless (Name of Leader) he/she walks through their own grief process. Please allow (Name of Leader) to take the time they need to cope so that they will not lose his/her hope.

As my leader continues to lead while grieving, help those

he/she leads to show compassion and grace in this season of (Name of Leader) life.

Help us to extend to (Name of Leader) the same amount of grace that we often expect and demand from (Name of Leader)

Give my leader peace of mind, if he/she needs to take an extended break.

Allow my leader to come back healed, refreshed, refueled and in recovery mode at the right time.

Thank you Lord, for Victory over Death.

In Jesus' Name Amen.

Amen

Prayer for Anyone Walking Through Loss of a Loved One

Dear Lord,

Thank you for my life and for the life of my loved one (Name Your Loved One) who has passed away due to COVID-19.

I thank you for all the memories I now cherish and for the legacy of (Name Your Loved One)

As I grieve please help me to do so effectively.

As I grieve, help me not to lose hope for my future.

As I grieve, help me to move forward in faith and love knowing that's what (Name of Your Loved One) would want.

If by chance I ever get to a point where it feels as though I can't handle the grief anymore, please help me to allow someone else to help me through my pain so that I can truly recover.

Amen

Prayer for Anyone Who Has Experienced Unexpected Job Loss

Dear Lord,

Help me to cope and not lose hope in the midst of my challenging situation. Please bless my family and my finances as we attempt to live with a decrease in income.

Help me and my family to not be embarrassed or

ashamed to connect with churches, nonprofit organizations and even other government agencies that may be able to provide food and help with our bills.

As I look for a new job, please direct me so that I may find even a temporary job online. Give me wisdom and insight regarding how I might be able to make money on my own as an independent contractor or starting a family business.

Help me not to give up, but to keep my head up knowing I am indeed doing the best I can to recover.

Amen

Prayer for Anyone Going Through Separation or Divorce

Dear Lord,

Help me as I mourn my broken marriage even though I never expected to feel this type of grief.

Help me not to be ashamed to admit that this hurts.

Please give me peace of mind and renewed hope for my future.

Help me not to get stuck trying to figure out how I could have changed my current circumstances.

Help me to move forward knowing things can and will get better.

Bless me and my children with a good support system.

Protect me, my finances and my new life and help me not to give up on my dreams or my destiny.

Amen

Global Prayer for Our World

Dear Lord,

Bless our world as we deal with the ramifications and results of COVID-19.

Bless the healthcare workers and the scientists and all those who are working diligently to win against COVID-19.

HELP, each Nation to do its part to help citizens to recover.

Comfort the families of the millions that have died due to

COVID-19.

Give us all patience, wisdom and compassion as unprecedented grief hovers over our world.

Bless our global economy and our future as we move forward in hope.

Amen

The Serenity Prayer *(Author Unknown)*

God grant me the serenity to accept the things I can not change.

The courage to change the things I can and the wisdom to know the difference.

7

GRIEF PHOTOTHERAPY

Anytime I'm interviewed or speak I often joke and tell people, Yes, there are black people in Nebraska! It's a running joke with black and brown folk in Nebraska and yes, it always makes people laugh. I say this to say though born in Winnfield, Louisiana my hometown is Omaha, Nebraska. It's where my parents migrated by the time I was 2.

It's my home. It's where I learned about life, love and crises and what it takes to win through life, no matter the circumstances. Over the years, like any family, we have had challenging times, yet through it all, I wouldn't change a thing about God's providence.

I am who I am today, because of what I learned and lived in a house full of faith, fortitude and tough love, led by Dewayne and Lillie Holmes. Whew!

These photos really provided therapy for me whenever I was able to go and review.

Omaha is the backdrop for the first 2 events and Winnfield is the backdrop for the latter.

Here are photos from 3 events: First, I'm sharing images from my sister's September 18, 2015 wedding in Omaha, Nebraska where photographers Perry Taylor and Alterick Wilson captured these wonderful images of my family's last BIG EVENT 4 months before my father Dewayne Holmes Sr. died. My sister and her husband Karmen & David Worley, honored my dad by incorporating Dewayne as their son's middle name in honor of my father. Enjoy these photos that always bring great joy to me and my family.

Photo of Baby David Dewayne Worley Captured by Photographer: Connie Lee Photography

I'm also sharing photos from my dad's Memorial Concert and Homegoing Funeral where Bryant McCain and team did an awesome job thoughtfully capturing the moments of joy and pain we experienced as we honored my father and said good-bye here on earth.

Lastly, I'm sharing photos from my grandmother Eleanor Nash Holmes' Homegoing in our hometown of Winnfield, Louisiana. *Images: Sabrina*

Worley Wedding Photos
September 18, 2015

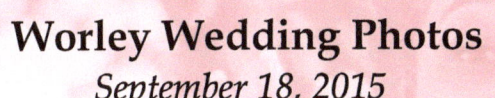

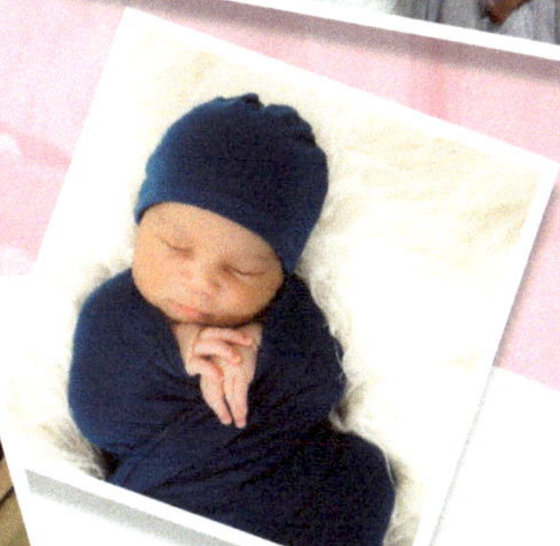

Grief Phototherapy 83

A Legacy of Service
DeWayne Holmes Sr : 1948 - 2016

84 *Grief Phototherapy*

A Century Fulfilled
Eleanor Nash Holmes : 1913 - 2015

Grief Phototherapy 85

DWANN HOLMES
Entrepreneur , Chaplain, Trainer-Consultant

Dwann loves Media, Marketing, Mentorship and Ministry. Her career started as a TV News Reporter/Anchor in 1994 and then she opened a Faith-Friendly TV Production Company in 2000 that transformed into an Ad Agency while living in Nashville, Tennessee. Dwann has experience as the Director of Marketing at the University of Nebraska at Kearney. Her entrepreneurial spirit has allowed her to own and operate D&C Multi Media. Dwann currently owns and

operates a 19-year media and training company called Dwann & Company where she functions as a Chief Strategist.

Dwann is an award-winning journalist, nominated for a few Emmys, was named a TOP 30 Future Leader by Ebony Magazine in 2000 and most recently made her way to the top of Amazon's Best Sellers.

She combines her multi-media expertise to help others in the personal and professional growth and development. Her specialties include: Marketing, Business Development, Media Training, Media Campaign Development, Public Speaking, Creative Concept Development, Creating and Launching Brand Awareness, Media Account Development and Management, and Online Marketing and Staff Development.

Dwann's roots stem from Omaha, Nebraska. She attended the University of Nebraska at Kearney with a degree in Broadcast Journalism with a minor in Sports Communications.

Dwann is a leading force in prophetic ministry and loves helping college students, single moms and entrepreneurs WIN THROUGH CRISIS!

Dwann is an engaging speaker who connects with people of all ages, backgrounds and ethnicities. As a mother of bi-racial children she has a heart to educate those in corporate America and education regarding racial sensitivity and acceptance. As a seasoned media professional she is often called upon to lend expertise and thoughts on calamities that often happen when media isn't monitored properly. As an Inspirational speaker, Dwann loves encouraging people to embrace their authentic self. She also delivers powerful messages on VISION-CASTING and the POWER OF THE MIND! Her upcoming book GET BACK UP! details Dwann's journey from pain to purpose after encountering what seemed like the most devastating crisis of her life.

For media and podcast interviews please visit BookDwann.com or email wecare@globalpropheticinstitute.com For Urgent Requests Text 877.595.9117

ORDER TODAY

Available at
amazon

amazon.com   amazonkindle

PASTOR
Rosemary Winbush

Kairos International
Minister, Speaker, Author, and Trainer,
Success Coach and Life Builder for
Children's Ministry Leader's and Workers,
Families, Church Leaders, People

Essentials to
Start Build and Refresh
Children's Ministry

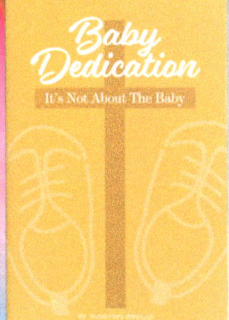

Baby Dedication:
It's Not About the Baby

Bible SnapShot:
Journey Through the Word

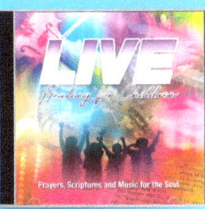

Live Healing
for Children

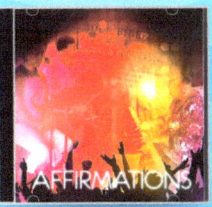

Affirmations

Available at amazon

www.rosemarywinbush.com

www.ingramcontent.com/pod-product-compliance
Lightning Source LLC
Chambersburg PA
CBHW042330150426
43194CB00001B/11